Katelyn Rice

The Spanish-American WAR

Consultants

Dorothy Levin, M.S.Ed., MBA
St. Lucie County Schools

Vanessa Ann Gunther, Ph.D.
Department of History
Chapman University

Cassandra Slone
Pinellas County Public Schools

Publishing Credits

Rachelle Cracchiolo, M.S.Ed., *Publisher*
Conni Medina, M.A.Ed., *Managing Editor*
Emily R. Smith, M.A.Ed., *Series Developer*
Diana Kenney, M.A.Ed., NBCT, *Content Director*
Courtney Patterson, *Multimedia Designer*

Image Credits: pp.4, 5 (bottom), 7 (top), 8-9, 16-17, 17 (top), 19 (top), 31 State Archives of Florida; p.5 LOC [g3860.ar140500]; pp.6-7 Niday Picture Library/Alamy; pp.10-11 Look and Learn / Bridgeman Images; p.11 (right) Wikimedia Commons/Public Domain, (left) Public Domain; pp.13, 29 North Wind Picture Archives; pp.12-13 Niday Picture Library/Alamy; pp.14-15 State Archives of Florida/Willets; p.15 (top) ullstein bild / Granger, NYC; pp.18-19, 24 (bottom), 29 (top and middle) Niday Picture Library/Alamy; pp.21 (bottom) U.S. Office of Federal Management; pp.22-23 US Army/National Archives/ The LIFE Picture Collection/Getty Images; p.23 LOC [LC-USZ62-48331]; pp.24 (top), 32 Timothy Hughes Rare & Early Newspapers; p.25 OurDocuments.gov; p.26 iStock. com/Juanmonino; p.27 (bottom) Sven Creutzmann/ Mambo photo/Getty Images, (top) Kamira / Shutterstock. com; p.28 Interim Archives/Getty Images; p.29 (bottom) US Army/National Archives/The LIFE Picture Collection/ Getty Images; all other images from iStock and/or Shutterstock.

Library of Congress Cataloging-in-Publication Data

Names: Rice, Katelyn.
Title: The Spanish-American War / Katelyn Rice.
Description: Huntington Beach, CA : Teacher Created Materials, Inc., 2017. |
  Series: The United States at war | Includes index.
Identifiers: LCCN 2016014355 (print) | LCCN 2016017461 (ebook) | ISBN
  9781493835416 (pbk.) | ISBN 9781480756885 (eBook)
Subjects: LCSH: Spanish-American War, 1898--Juvenile literature.
Classification: LCC E715 .R495 2017 (print) | LCC E715 (ebook) | DDC
  973.8/9--dc23
LC record available at https://lccn.loc.gov/2016014355

Teacher Created Materials

5301 Oceanus Drive
Huntington Beach, CA 92649-1030
http://www.tcmpub.com

ISBN 978-1-4938-3541-6
© 2017 Teacher Created Materials, Inc.

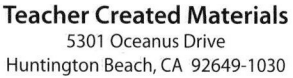

Table of Contents

Life Before the War

In the 1890s, many people in Florida were pioneers. They came from other states to make new homes. Many of them left all of their things behind to start a new life. They wanted to discover new areas of the country. Some of those people started small tobacco farms. Some started citrus farms. Some raised animals. New towns were built. Churches and schools were erected.

Little did they know that only 90 miles away, a war was brewing in Cuba. Cuba is an island country that is not far from the United States. It has rolling hills and white sandy beaches. Back then, Cuba was a Spanish **colony**. It belonged to Spain. Cuba wanted to be its own country, but Spain did not want that to happen.

This Florida home was built in 1894.

Gilded Age

The 1890s in America were part of the Gilded Age. It was a time when many people were getting rich, crime was often unpunished, and social norms were changing. Industry in Florida was rapidly expanding as railroads made the area more accessible.

Leading to War

Tensions started rising in Cuba long before the 1890s. Cubans were fed up with Spain. They didn't like the high **taxes** they had to pay. They didn't like the way Spain ran the Cuban government. They felt that they were being denied certain rights. In 1868, a group of Cuban planters **revolted**. The fight lasted for ten years. It became known as the Ten Years' War. The war ended with no clear winner. Spain still ruled Cuba but promised to make changes.

During this time, many Cubans moved to Florida. They wanted to live in a safer place. They wanted better jobs. They liked the lower taxes in Florida. So, they brought their skills. They used their strong business sense to set up factories. Cigar factories, in particular, became commonplace in Florida.

1869 sketch of the Cuban Revolution

a cigar shop in Key West, Florida

Taking the Lead

Many people fought for Cuba's freedom. One of those people was José Martí. He was a poet and an **activist**. He wrote essays and poems that called for freedom for Cuban landowners. Spain did not like his efforts to unite the Cuban rebels. He was **deported** to Spain in 1871.

Martí continued to write in Spain. He also earned his masters of arts and law degrees. His writing took him to France, Guatemala, and Mexico. Finally, he went back to Cuba in 1878. He was **exiled** back to Spain a year later. But, this did not end his quest.

José Martí

Martí shared his thirst for freedom with other people. Paulina Pedroso fought beside Martí in Florida. She was a black leader. She was also a business owner in the state. She worked to end segregation in Tampa. Martí lived with her family for a while. The two leaders raised money for weapons for Cuban rebels. They inspired people to fight for freedom.

Paulina Pedroso

Paulina Pedroso's parents were slaves. But she was born free in Cuba in 1845. Slavery had ended in Latin America before it did in North America.

Martí poses in front of the Vicente Martínez Ybor (EE-bohr) cigar factory, where he made one of his most famous speeches.

As the years passed, neither Spain nor Cuba worked out their problems. In 1896, Spain's leaders sent someone to crush the Cuban rebels. His name was General Valeriano Weyler y Nicolau. He was made governor of Cuba. He took swift action. He wanted to make sure the rebels were set apart from civilians. So, he started his "Reconcentration Plan."

Weyler put civilians in camps. There, they were controlled by the Spanish army. They could not help the rebels. They could not revolt. People had eight days to make their way to the camps. They were killed if they did not show up. About 400,000 Cubans were sent to the camps by 1898. Food was sparse. Living conditions were poor. Disease spread quickly. Hundreds of thousands of people died.

Weyler's plan made his military goals easier to reach. But he lost support from many countries, such as the United States.

Cubans are forced to move to a reconcentration camp.

THE BUTCHER OF CUBA

Weyler in His Ferocious and Frivolous Moods
--Origin of Reconcentrado Plan.

ACCORDING TO HIS OWN WORDS, HE CARED ONLY TO SUBDUE
THE INSURRECTION, NO MATTER AT WHAT COST OF BLOOD
AND MONEY—SHUT UP THE CUBAN PEASANTRY AND LET
THEM STARVE LIKE SHEEP IN PENS—HOW HE BULLIED
PRESS CORRESPONDENTS.

Gen. Valeriano Weyler.

General Weyler

Weyler's Nickname

Americans were horrified when they read about Weyler's tactics in the newspapers. These tactics quickly earned him the nickname the Butcher.

Gaining Support

After hearing about Weyler's tactics, many people in the United States backed Cuba's fight against Spain. They gave money. Some joined the armed forces. They were upset by the stories about Weyler's camps. But, the United States had not declared war on Spain.

In early 1898, the United States sent a ship to Cuba. The USS *Maine* would make sure that the country's people and property in Cuba were safe. On February 15, the USS *Maine* calmly sat in the harbor. Suddenly, the ship exploded and quickly sank. About 266 of the 354 crewmembers died. The cause of the blast was unknown. The captain believed that the ship's boiler exploded. But many people blamed Spain. That was enough to convince President McKinley to declare war in April 1898. The Spanish-American War had begun.

Men clean up the wreckage of the USS *Maine* in 1898.

USS New York

During the Spanish-American War, the U.S. Navy used armored cruisers. The USS *New York* was one of them. It cost $3.5 million to make this ship. That was a lot of money in 1888!

Florida was very important in the war. It was close to Cuba. Its location made it the best place to house soldiers. As a result, many military bases opened in the state. Tampa had the main base. The city of Lakeland was used for even more troops. Key West was another important base in the state. Soon, these cities were teeming with people.

A group of Cuban **immigrants** also offered to help the United States fight. They were known as the Army of the Cuban Republic. Many of them had been cigar makers in Florida. The other half of the group was from New York. There were 390 of them in all. They set sail for Cuba on a ship called the *Florida* in May 1898.

members of the Army of the Cuban Republic

When they arrived in Cuba, they saw small towns. Around the towns were vast areas of farmland. There was cotton, tobacco, and sugarcane. Many of the towns were run down. Most of the crops had been ruined. The land had been ravaged during the time of the reconcentration camps.

Digging for Victory

Soldiers used trench warfare in the Spanish-American War. In trench warfare, soldiers dig, hide in, and shoot from long trenches. The trenches provide protection and give troops a safe place to sleep and eat.

During the War

Many people moved to Florida during the war. Some who moved there were soldiers. Many brought their families with them. Cubans moved there, too. They were trying to escape the problems in their home country. Some cities grew rapidly in just one year! The growing number of people helped the state's economy prosper. There were now more people to spend money in the state.

The war impacted the state's economy in other ways, too. The cigar industry boomed. Tobacco was grown in Cuba. Tobacco leaves and finished cigars were sent to Florida. People in Florida sold them for a profit. This brought money into the state. Cigars became one of the state's specialties.

Wanish Cigar Factory employees in the late 1800s

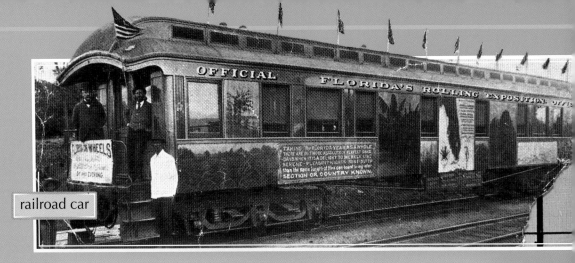

railroad car

Railroads were also built in the state after the war. This helped with trade. Goods could now get where they needed to go. Railroads also helped move people. Both goods and people could get where they needed to go in a timely manner.

Florida soon became home to many Cubans. People traveled across the ocean to get to the state. Many of them moved to the same areas. They settled in towns, such as Key West, Tampa, and Miami. They wanted to form tight-knit communities outside of their home country. These towns offered people a sense of security. People spoke the same language. They enjoyed the same foods.

People brought their **customs**, traditions, and beliefs with them from Cuba. They were able to hold on to their culture. The culture of Florida started to merge with that of its new residents. Over time, Cuban culture became part of Florida's way of life.

Key West in 1900

Cuban restaurant
in Key West

Tampa

Miami

Key West

Faces of the War

Some of the most well-known heroes of the war joined forces in Florida. One such hero was Theodore Roosevelt. He led a team of soldiers called the **Rough Riders**. The team was made up of men from all over the country. There were cowboys and athletes. There were gold **prospectors** and American Indians, too.

Theodore Roosevelt and the Rough Riders

The Rough Riders got orders to leave Tampa on June 5, 1898. This was no easy task. Roosevelt called the loading of troops onto transports "higglety-pigglety business." The port was packed with 17,000 soldiers all trying to leave for Cuba at once. Anyone or anything that didn't fit was left behind—including horses.

The Rough Riders finally left on June 14. They made it to Cuba on June 22. On July 1, 1898, they found success. The troops quickly overtook Kettle Hill. The troops pressed on and conquered San Juan Hill. Two days later, U.S. warships were able to destroy the Spanish fleet. This led to the Spanish surrender just two weeks later.

Remarkable Roosevelt

As a child and young adult, Theodore Roosevelt was very sick. He had severe **asthma**, a condition that makes it hard to breathe. Despite the advice of his doctor, Roosevelt pushed himself to get stronger. He adopted an active lifestyle. He called it "strenuous living."

Another group of heroes who fought in the war were the **Buffalo Soldiers**. The group was made up of African Americans. They were largely responsible for the American success at San Juan Hill and were supported by the Rough Riders. But they didn't just fight the Spanish. They also fought racism. They weren't treated as equals on the battlefield. Still, they fought. After they won, a Rough Rider named William "Frank" Knox said, "I never saw braver men anywhere."

Racism

In the 1890s, Southern states passed laws to prevent African Americans from voting. They put black students in separate schools. Slavery was against the law, but hatred was still rampant.

This 1874 cartoon depicts a black voter trying to cast his ballot in the South.

Nurses were also essential to the war effort. They were needed on the battle lines. So, the military asked women to help. Many had already been trained as nurses. About 1,500 women served as nurses during the war. They treated injuries and illnesses. Dr. Anita Newcomb McGee was made assistant surgeon general of the U.S. Army during the war. She was the only woman allowed to wear an officer's uniform.

Anita Newcomb McGee

Buffalo Soldiers

End of the War

A cease-fire was signed on August 12, 1898. The United States and Spain signed the **Treaty** of Paris four months later. The treaty ended the Spanish-American War. As part of the deal, Spain agreed to stop fighting. Spanish forces would leave Cuba. Cubans would govern themselves. Spain would also give two of its colonies—Guam and Puerto Rico—to the United States. But the deal didn't stop there. The United States bought the Philippines from Spain, too. The country paid $20 million for the island nation.

Spanish and U.S. leaders sign the Treaty of Paris in 1898.

U.S. troops stayed in Cuba for several years after the war ended. They helped set up new schools. They studied illnesses. They looked for cures for yellow fever.

In 1901, the United States and Cuba signed the Platt Amendment. The United States agreed to pull its troops out of Cuba. In return, the country would be allowed to use Cuban land for military purposes. And, Cuba would not be allowed to give any other country power over its land and people. This contract stayed in effect until 1934.

Platt Amendment

Life After the War

The U.S. armed forces helped Cubans win their fight for freedom. Men and women stood bravely when faced with the dangers of war. They cared for the sick and wounded. They fought for causes they believed in.

In the years that followed, Florida stayed a center of Cuban American culture. Cuban Americans share their culture with their communities. They inspire people through art and dance. They are active in politics. They play vital roles in education. They help shape America.

Cuban restaurant in Miami

Sequence It!

The Spanish-American War is often not given much attention in history books. By describing its causes and effects, we can help other people know more about this war.

Create a time line that shows the causes and effects of the war. Be sure to show which major events led to others.

Glossary

activist—a person who uses or supports strong actions, such as protests, to make changes

asthma—a condition that makes it difficult to breathe

Buffalo Soldiers—African American soldiers who served the United States's armed forces in the period after the Civil War

colony—an area ruled by a country far away

customs—traditional behaviors or actions of a group of people

deported—to force someone who is not a citizen to leave a country

exiled—forced to leave a native country for political reasons

immigrants—people who come to a country to live there

prospectors—people who search an area for gold, minerals, and oil

revolted—fought in a violent way against a leader or government

Rough Riders—the members of the cavalry organized by Theodore Roosevelt during the Spanish-American War

taxes—money that people are required to pay to a government

treaty—a formal agreement made between two or more countries or groups

Index

Your Turn!

PEACE TREATY IS SIGNED

Negotiations at Paris Concluded at Last.

A SCENE FOR A PAINTER

SIGNATURES ATTACHED TO THE GREAT DOCUMENT.

SPANIARDS ARE MUCH CAST DOWN

The Final Incident In the War of Diplomacy Witnessed Between Eight and Nine O'clock Saturday Evening In the Stately Chamber of the French Foreign Office. The Treaty Sealed With the French Tricolor—A Demand For the Pens As Souvenirs.

By Associated Press.
Paris, Dec. 11.—The treaty of peace

A Different Perspective

This newspaper conveys U.S. reaction to the end of the Spanish-American War. What words stand out to you? What is the tone? How might Spain's newspaper headlines have differed? Write a newspaper article about the peace treaty from Spain's perspective.